Maya Mythology

Myths and Folklore of the Mayan Civilization

Table of Contents

Introduction

At some point, the Mayan civilization was the most culturally rich and sophisticated in the world. They excelled in the fields of art, astronomy, math, and architecture, not to mention developing one of the world's earliest writing systems—the logosyllabic script. Also known as Maya glyphs or script, this was a highly developed writing system in the pre-Columbian Americas. The Mayan civilization occupied Mesoamerica, a historic area encompassing central Mexico, Belize, Guatemala, and parts of El Salvador and Honduras.

From about 300 B.C. to the 1500s, the Mayan people prospered and established one of the most significant civilizations in human history, up until the Spanish conquest. However, those peoples of varying cultures didn't actually call themselves 'Maya.' This is a modern term coined to refer to the collective peoples who dwelled in those areas and shared many cultural and historical similarities. For centuries, the Mayan people developed agriculture techniques and farmed crops associated with that region, like chili peppers, beans, and maize. Around 750 B.C., the first Mayan cities were established, paving the way for some of the fascinating architecture the world has ever seen, with many buildings surviving to this very day and inspiring awe and admiration.

The Mayan people built large temples and monuments, and they established major cities that were cultural and central hubs for thousands of people from across the region. They created trade networks and had a complex political system with major rivalries between kingdoms and regions. For many years, the Mayans dwelled in the region and prospered, but with the advent of the Spaniards, their civilization quickly collapsed. By 1697, the last of the Mayan cities fell to the conquest, and the Maya civilization was no more.

Many Mayan peoplewere literate, mostly the richer nobles. They leveraged their glyphs to record their history and knowledge in screen fold books, with only a handful of which are sadly still around.

Despite the Mayans' immense advancement in architecture and building, arts, and political systems, it wouldn't be an overstatement to say that their greatest asset was their ability to tell stories.

The Mayan people were natural storytellers, and their imagination knew no bounds. They took the traditional Mesoamerican versions of creation and the gods of the universe and molded them into their own, adding and shaping their unique version of mythology and folktales. This left us with a significant pantheon of gods and goddesses, each with a memorable and captivating story. The Mayans had an image of the universe and their place in it, and they told stories of gods and heroes that rival Greek Mythology.

At first glance, Mayan mythology can be confusing. Gods took different forms and had varying names. Heroes were told in different contexts across regions and their stories varied, sometimes greatly. Yet, if you look beyond the haze, you'll find that there was an established universe with specific gods. Yes, they might have had different names in city-states than the farther regions, but it wasn't the name that mattered; it was the type of god and what they represented and symbolized to their people. These gods were not just there to be worshipped and venerated. They played a significant role in keeping the peace and maintaining harmony in the Mayan world, and for that, they were respected and honored.

This book will explore Mayan mythology and the vast pantheon of gods and deities that this proud and smart person has worshipped for centuries. We will also look into folk tales and see what it means to be a hero for the Mayan people and what those ordinary humans did to earn the kind of respect and veneration that kept their names mentioned in song and tale for a long time.

Chapter One:

Creation

Like with all mythology, creation came first. Before there were gods and heroes, there was nothingness. We know the origins of everything and the early players in a particular culture that affect everything that comes after them through creation stories. For the Mayans, the story of creation is outlined in the Popol Vuh, also known as Popol Wuj in the K'iche' language. The Popol Vuh is a sacred Mayan text that explains the history of the K'iche' people and recounts the origins of humankind. It specifically focuses on the K'iche' people as it was documented by the royal lineage of the K'iche' that once upon a time rules the Guatemalan highlands—the K'iche' also dwelled in Mexican states like Chiapas and Yucatan as well as some places in Belize and Honduras.

The closest translation to Popol Vuh is 'book of the community,' and true to that translation, it gives an account of the Mayan story of creation, the K'iche' lineages, the tale of the Hero Twins, and land rights. We will focus on the K'iche' story of creation, but it's important to understand that there are different versions in the Mayan civilization for how their world was created. For the K'iche', thirteen gods helped create the first humans out of maize. For the Yucatec, on the other hand, only two gods were involved in creation. Despite the variation, the essence of both versions is pretty much the same. Even the gods struggled to create, not very much unlike humans who also face many challenges in their attempt to create, whether it's life or anything else. Moreover, both versions highlight that life comes from earth since humans were created from maize—corn was very important in the Mayan diet. This is why the earth is always revered and honored in Mayan culture.

An excerpt from the Popol Vuh, translated by Dennis Tedlock, says, "There is not yet one person, one animal, bird, fish, crab, tree, rock, hollow, canyon, meadow, forest. Only the sky alone is there; the face of the earth is not clear. Only the sea alone is pooled under all the sky; there is nothing whatever gathered together... Whatever might be is simply not there: only murmurs, ripples, in the dark, in the night. Only the Maker, Modeler alone, the Sovereign Plumed Serpent, the Bearers, Begetters are in the water, a glittering light. They are there; they are enclosed in quetzal feathers, in blue-green... So, there were three of them, as Heart of Sky, who came to the Sovereign Plumed Serpent when the dawn of life was conceived: 'How should the sowing be, and the dawning? Who is to be the provider, nurturer?' 'Let it be this way, think about it: this water should be removed, emptied out for the formation of the earth's own plate and platform, then should come the sowing, the dawning of the 'sky-earth'... And then the earth arose because of them; it was simply their word that brought it forth. For the forming of the earth, they said 'Earth.' It arose suddenly, just like a cloud, like a mist, now forming, unfolding. Then the mountains were separated from the water; all at once, the great mountains came forth... Now they planned the animals of the mountains, all the guardians of the forest, creatures of the mountains: the deer, birds, pumas, jaguars, serpents, rattlesnakes, fer-de-lances, guardians of the bushes... And then the deer and birds were told by the Maker, Modeler, Bearer, Begetter: 'Talk, speak out. Don't moan, don't cry out… Name now our names, praise us. We are your mother; we are your father'… But it didn't turn out that they spoke like people: they just squawked, they just chattered, they just howled… They had not heard their speech among the animals; it did not come to fruition, and it was not complete. And so, their flesh was brought low: they served, they were eaten, they were killed– the animals on the face of the earth…."

This excerpt from the 'book of the community' sums up the story of creation for the K'iche' people. The story starts with Huracan, the 'Heart of the Sky,' who was a K'iche' God of wind, fire, and storm. Along with other deities like Kukulkan (also known as Gukumatz or the Feathered Serpent), he wanted to create humans with hearts and minds that could 'keep the days' and worship them. They wanted to make creations that looked like them to honor their legacy, but such an endeavor was not easy. In other versions of the story, there were two main gods before the world was created: Gukumatz and Tepeu. It is said the world around them was covered in darkness, but the gods glistened with colorful feathers of blue and green. Together, they decided to create the world just as fast as they could think of it.

When Gukumatz and Tepeu thought of earth, it was created. Lands formed and filled the dark world, filling it up with mountains, trees, valleys, and anything else they could think of. They thought of the sky, and it came to be, and thus, the earth as we know it was formed. The gods decided that they needed creatures to fill the vast earth they've created and worship them. The deities, or the Creators, failed on their first attempt. They created animals first, but they could not worship them or keep the days. They started with deer, serpents, panthers, and birds, along with countless other beasts that we know today. The creators commanded their creations to praise their names. "Say our names," they ordered, but the animals only squawked and chattered. They tried to obey their Creators, but they could not. The beasts' noise was so annoying as they tried to praise the Creators, the gods ordered them to stop.

"How else can we be invoked and remembered on the face of the earth? We have already made our first try at our work and design, but it turned out that they didn't keep our days, nor did they glorify us," said the Creators. They tried a second time, using earth and mud this time to make the bodies. Their second attempt also failed, and the bodies couldn't sustain themselves, and they disintegrated and dissolved. On the third try, they used wood, and they succeeded and were pleased with their creation for a short while. This second race of men was able to talk, walk, and even multiply.

"They came into being; they multiplied, they had daughters, they had sons, these manikins, wood-carvings. But there was nothing in their hearts and nothing in their minds, no memory of their mason and builder. They just went and walked wherever they wanted. Now they did not remember the Heart of Sky."

Despite taking the time to create humans with hearts and minds, the Creators forgot one very important thing—the soul. Their creations had no souls; their words were empty and meaningless. Worst of all, though, they quickly lost interest in worshipping the gods and were no longer loyal to their Creators. This could not stand. The Creators sent a great flood to destroy their creation. There are different versions as to why the flood was sent down. It might have been because the humans neglected their duty to worship and praise the gods. Some versions say that the world was old and tired after the Creators' several attempts to fill it with creatures, and it needed to be renewed. A few versions claim that the reason for the Great Flood is transgressions committed by humans like cannibalism. Other variations have Christian influences from the Spanish conquest era, citing the transgression that begot the flood was a man killing his brother, namely, Cain and Able.

Whatever the reason for the flood was, in the Mayan retelling of creation, it happened. The gods also commanded the animals on earth to attack the survivors, and the beasts complied. Their heads were ripped off, and their limbs were separated from their bodies. Those who survived had molten pitch fall on them, destroying their bodies until there was nothing left. It is said that a few managed to escape and fled to the woods where they were turned into monkeys, living proof for the following generations of humans of the punishment the gods can inflict for the worshippers who fail to praise the gods.

Gukumatz and Tepeu and the other creators still wanted a race of humans with enough intellect and heart to worship them. It is said that the first two fought for a long time on how to move forward and how they could finally make a race of man in the shape they truly wanted. One version of the creation myth states that a man and his dog survived the great flood. One day, the dog took the shape of a woman. Together, the man and woman procreated and repopulated the world, and the creators were pleased with their offspring. However, the most common version is that, after a long time of deliberation, the gods were stuck, unable to find an answer to their dilemma. Then, one day, the animals brought them a stack of corn that grew on the other side of the planet. The creators liked the new material and found it suitable for creating a new race of man, their fourth attempt.

This new race of man was perfect in every way the gods wanted. They didn't disintegrate like the first race of men out of mud, and they weren't soulless and meaningless like those made out of wood.

They were strong, and their minds were developed, filled with thoughts, and they had felt that they could put into words. The first thing they did after their creation was praising the gods and thanking them for the gift of life they had been given. "This time, the beings shaped by the gods are everything they hoped for and more: not only do the first four men pray to their makers, but they have perfect vision and therefore perfect knowledge," says the Popol Vuh. There were four men first, the first of their kind.

The gods asked the first men what they saw, and they replied, "We can see forever, through rocks and trees and mountains to the edges of the earth. We can see and understand everything." This made the gods nervous. They worried that their creation may have been too perfect, which meant they might rival the gods themselves. This was not the purpose of those creatures, who were only created to worship and honor the gods. And thus, Gukumatz and Tepeu took some of the humans' vision and limited their ability to only see what was in front of them. With this next experiment with creation, the humans couldn't see above and through things, and their vision was limited, which meant that their knowledge of the world was limited and could never rival the gods'.

The gods created women for the men to take as wives, and from those eight, the lineage of K'iche' came and still exists to this very day. Despite being deprived of some of their abilities, the new race of man continues to worship and praise the gods, grateful for what they had rather than what they had lost. So, as it was, a man came from white and yellow corn, a result of several attempts at creation by the Creators. The first several attempts did not work, and when the gods finally got it right, they took away some of man's power to keep us from rivaling them. A lot of parallels can be drawn between creation myths in Islam and Christianity. If you look closely, you can find many similarities between the different belief systems on how the world was created.

There are also many similarities between Mayan and Greek mythology. For example, in some versions of the tale of creation, survivors of the great flood challenged the gods and lit a fire. As punishment, they were all turned into animals. This is very similar to Greek mythology, where Prometheus stole the fire and gave it to the humans, who were then punished when Pandora's Box unleashed all the evils of the world upon them.

One more thing to remember when it comes to the creation myth in the Mayan culture is the importance of the spoken word. Some believe that the early gods Gukumatz and Tepeu filled the world with dialogue. They didn't just think of something to create it; they said it. This shows us the importance of language in the Mayan culture, which then went on to develop the most sophisticated writing system of the ancient world. For the people of those areas, the Mayans, the value of an object shows when you give it a name. Another way to think about it is that the Mayans have it the other way around: objects are named, and then they come to life, unlike everywhere else where an object initially exists and then is given a name. According to the Popol Vuh, that wasn't the case.

The gods created the earth and the plants, but it wasn't enough for them because there was no dialogue, no words being spoken. This is why they created the animal in an attempt to create intelligent beings that can use words and express their thoughts. When the animals couldn't do what they were created for, they were banished to the forests, never to leave unless to serve more intelligent beings—the humans. The later races of man that were created reflected the gods' great care about the spoken word and the importance of language. Humans are vocal creatures who communicate through words, and it is because we were created by gods that put a great deal of interest into the spoken word.

The creation myth concludes that the early humans multiplied and filled the earth, but the sun was not yet created, so they were destined to roam the earth in utter darkness. They tried to migrate east in search of a source of light, but there were none. Tired, starved, and desperate, the early humans prayed to the gods and asked for their help, which moved the Creators. The sun soon rose from the sky, and the humans' prayers were answered. Soon, they managed to find warmth in the sun's light and use it to farmlands with many crops, including maize, the materials from which they were made.

Chapter Two:

Gods and Goddesses

If the Mayan story of creation tells us one thing, it's that the gods were held in great regard by the Mayans. They weren't just omniscient deities that people prayed to and honored. The gods and goddesses were involved in every aspect of the Mayans' lives. They brought harvest and rain, blessing people with or denying them crops. They controlled the weather and were there when you died just as they were at birth. The Mayan gods even chose your mate for you. There wasn't an aspect of a Mayan's life that didn't involve the god in one way or the other.

In many paintings, the gods were believed to be cross-eyed, and for that, the Mayan mothers would dangle a bead from their kids' forehead just to make them in the image of the cross-eyed gods and honor them. The veneration of the gods didn't just include small gestures like this. The Mayans, especially the richer nobles, would dress as the gods as often as possible. Even in their architecture, the Mayans tried to build cities and construct buildings in a way they knew would please the gods. For example, the Temple of Kukulcán (also known as La Pirámide) was built to honor the god Kukulkan, the feathered serpent. The temple was designed with steep stairs that connect the temple at the top to the base, where a stone serpent head lies. On the twin equinoxes every year, the temple is designed so that a shadow is cast, that of a serpent moving the stairs of the temple toward the serpent head. This creates an image of a serpent slowly descending to earth. This tribute to Kukulkan is to honor one of the most popular Maya gods, and to this very day, many still make the pilgrimage to the temple twice a year to receive the god's blessing and honor him.

This was just an example of one temple built for one god, but there are over 200 gods and goddesses in the Mayan pantheon, many of whom were honored in designs and architecture. Unfortunately, over time, we lost much of the knowledge about the deities worshipped by the Mayans for centuries. This was partly due to Bishop Diego de Landa burning much of the Mayan legacy and books in 1562.

He sought to destroy not just books, but also images, paintings, and any other implements of forcibly converted Mayans after the Spanish conquest. Fortunately, the Popol Vuh was one of the few surviving Mayan religious texts that gave us insight into which gods the Mayans worshipped. As explained earlier, this mainly covers the deities for the K'iche'. For other sects of Mayans, these gods might have been known by other names. In any case, there are many gods that we don't know of, and there are also quite a few that Christianity might have influenced, so they may not be the most accurate representation of Mayan gods worshipped during that time.

The pantheon of Mayan gods generally evolved over time, and they changed genders and nature from one version to the other, so it's important to keep that in mind. We'll explore some of the most popular gods during the Mayan eras and what their stories are.

Acan

In Mayan culture, Acan is the god of wine and intoxication. His name was often associated with a brew called Balche, which is a strong mead made from honey. Some translations of his name mean 'belch,' and he was always associated with partying and drinking. He is also said to be connected to Bohr (or Bol), a Lacandon Maya god of drunkenness. Acan was exciting and fun for the Mayans, and he liked to clown around and be the boisterous one among the other gods. The Mayans worshipped Acan, and they got close to him by drinking a lot. If you wanted to establish a connection with Acan, you had to get completely drunk and intoxicated. Only then, Acan might reveal himself to you. Some Mayans even took additional substances to further intoxicate themselves, like mushrooms or tobacco.

It's worth noting that wine was introduced by the Spanish conquerors, though, despite it being associated with Acan. The main drink the Mayans used to get drunk was Balche, which they were very good at making. The custom of getting intoxicated and drinking all night to get closer to Acan may be found in some places in central America today where Mayan gods like Acan are still revered. The Mayans used to take their drinking seriously, though. It is said that those who threw up had to wear their own vomit around their necks in bags for the rest of the evening. Acan was also associated with Cacoch, the god of creation and creativity, and the two of them were said to be drinking buddies.

Itzamná

Itzamná was one of the most powerful and important gods in Mayan culture. He was the ruler and king of heaven, day and night, blessed with vast knowledge and wisdom. Some say this is why he was often portrayed as an old man, sometimes without teeth. An important figure in Mayan culture, he is believed to have set the foundations of the Mayan civilization, giving humans the gift of writing and introducing them to the calendar to keep the time. It is also said that he appeared as four deities by the name Itzamnás, engulfing the world. The four gods were associated with the four directions and their corresponding colors: west-black, south-yellow, east-red, and north-white.

Itzamná was a deity of medicine and healing, too, and many Mayans prayed to him for healing and good health. He was sometimes associated with other deities like the creator, Hunab Ku and the sun god, Kinich Ahau. Itzamná has different roles and duties across eras. He was often referred to as a high priest and, at the same time, an upper god who resided in the sky on a celestial throne. He not only gave humans the gift of writing, but he also taught them about agriculture and hunting animals to feed themselves.

In other versions, Itzamná was called the Principal Bird Deity and was said to have the ability to transform into one. The bird he represented was often depicted holding a two-headed snake in its beak. There were several depictions of Itzamná as a bird deity, in some of which the bird's head looked like a bird of prey, and in others, a rain deity—some birds were believed to be bringers of rain like the laughing falcon. Itzamná, as a bird deity, was also thought to have control over the passage of time, each of its wings inscribed with signs for daylight and night. Itzamná was thought to use his transformative abilities to morph into human beings or at least bestow his grace upon them, as shown by the names of several kings of several ancient Maya cities whose names were a variation of his. Some kings were even buried with crowns or headdresses bearing the mark of the principal bird deity.

Acat

The Mayans were keen on tattooing and put a great deal of care into drawing the images or symbols of gods on their bodies, believing that doing so bestowed some of the god's power upon them or simply blessed them. Acat was the deity for tattooing in Mayan culture. The process of tattooing was intricate and important, so it was only reasonable that there was a god responsible for it. Acat blessed everything related to the tattooing process, including the needle, ink, and even the place where it took place. He also helped keep the artist's hands steady and inspired them to make the best tattoos.

Acat was given other names in Mayan culture like 'Ah Cat' or 'Ah Kat' and Acat-Cib. On the one hand, Acat meant reed, which is thought to be because hollow reeds were often used in the tattooing process. On the other hand, Ah Cat means 'he of the storage jar,' which is probably referencing the stored ink that was used for tattooing Mayans. In some variation of Mayan mythology, Acat was responsible for fetal growth and development, making sure that new life grows out of the womb of the old life. He is also sometimes considered one of the

Creators–the gods or deities responsible for the creation of humanity.

Despite the religious significance of tattoos for Mayans, it was a painful process, so not many Mayans stepped up to get tattooed. Those that did were considered brave and worthy of respect. Men would often get tattooed after marriage, and they got get tattooed anywhere. Women, on the other hand, often tattooed their upper body parts like the arms. For both men and women, Acat was the deity that helped them through the entire process. The artists, though, needed his help the most since the process was quite intricate and needed high accuracy to honor the gods with accurate depictions. So, artists would ask for Acat's blessing and guidance before making any tattoo.

Ah-Cuxtal

Speaking of newborns, Ah-Cuxtal was the god of birth in Mayan civilization. He was associated with safely delivering babies into the world is not just the physical sense, but also the spiritual one. Ah-Cuxtal's name literally translates to 'come to life,' which is what he helped do for newborns. Once Ah-Cuxtal was done with delivering a newborn, he would wash his hands clean and move on to deliver another child. The lord life-giver, Ah-Cuxtal, acting as the god of birth, is a bit odd since, in most civilizations, goddesses were usually responsible for that role, but Mayan civilization was always a bit different. Ah-Cuxtal was the one that protected the children and ensured their safe delivery into the world, and the Mayans worshiped and revered him for it.

Ah-Bolom-Tzacab

As Mayan civilization evolved, they became heavily invested in agriculture, and several crops became essential in the Mayan diet, like corn. It made sense that there is one or more gods responsible for watching over the crops and blessing the harvest. Ah-Bolom-Tzacab was that deity, the leafed-nose god of agriculture. He had several other names across regions and different eras of Mayan civilization like 'Ah Bolon Dz'acab. He was also considered a god of fertility since he was responsible for crops and, in some versions, even weather—especially lightning and rain since both affected agriculture.

Ah-Bolom-Tzacab was depicted as having a long nose similar to a bat, and in some variations, with a leaf coming out of his nose. He is said to have carried a torch or cigar, depending on the region and era of Mayan history. Ah-Bolom-Tzacab was also responsible for protecting the Mayan royal lineages not just by shielding them from danger, but he also helped pick the right lineage for the ruling class in Mayan civilization.

Ix Chel

Ix Chel was one of the most important goddesses in the Mayan civilization, associated with health, offspring, the weather, and in some stories, the moon. She was known to the early Mayans and has been portrayed in a variety of ways in Mayan culture. Ix Chel was sometimes young and attractive, a beautiful and seductive goddess. In other times, she was a wise old woman with infinite wisdom and knowledge and the power to destroy the world. Despite being often represented as the Moon Goddess, modern scholars question the assumption that Ix Chel is her.

Ix Chel was also associated with medicine and health, and she was celebrated and revered by shamans and Mayan doctors. They made tokens in her name and presented offerings so she could bless them with knowledge and wisdom to heal others. There are several tales on Ix Chel and her place in Mayan civilization. Some versions put her in the sky as the Moon Goddess, dwelling in the sky, and when she wasn't there, she lived in sinkholes filled with water.

It's interesting to see the contrast between the two versions of Ix Chel in Mayan culture: a young, seductive woman associated with the moon versus a crone with infinite power and the fate of the world in the palms of her hands. As mentioned, it's generally agreed that Ix Chel (also known as Goddess O) was an older woman, and she was married to Itzamna, making her one of the Creators. Goddess O is sometimes shown with beastly elements like jaguar claws and fangs coming out of her teeth. Her depictions often got grimmer, some showing her wearing a skirt of bones, symbolizing death and destruction. She is also sometimes associated with the Mayan god of rain Chaac, playing into flood portraits and images of great destruction.

Despite the grizzly depictions of Goddess O, her name sometimes translates to 'red rainbow," which might come as a surprise to some. But in Mayan culture, rainbows aren't colorful and a prelude to a good day or happy occurrence. Rainbows for the Mayans are a bad omen, sometimes referred to as flatulence of demons and other not-so-colorful descriptions.

Ahmucen-Cab

Also known as Ah Muzen Cab, this god was one of the creator gods who played a significant role in Mayan religious stories. He is often depicted as having the wings of the bee and is said to have been associated with the goddess of bee and honey, Colel Cab. Ah Muzen Cab is a god of honey, bees, and beekeeping. His role was important in Mayan cultures because honey was an integral component of Mesoamerican diets, and it was also quite a valuable trading commodity. Ah Muzen Cab is considered the descending god, portrayed in a unique upside-down position in portraits and statues. The temple of the descending god in Tulum is thought to be in honor of Ah Muzen Cab since Tulum was one of the most important places for his worshippers.

Ah Muzen Cab's role in creation is just one part of his story. According to the Chilam Balam version of creation, he blindfolded and covered the faces of the thirteen gods of day and allowed them to be captured by the nine gods of night. Ah Muzen Cab then took advantage of the darkness, planted seeds, and started building across the land, shaping it however he pleased. It's believed, though, that his creation was undone by the Bacabs—the four brother gods holding the sky at the four cardinal points of the compass.

Kukulkan

We already mentioned Kukulkan several times as he was one of the most revered and significant of the Mayan gods in the pantheon. The feathered serpent god is often considered to be the one that shaped the world as we know it today, and he created the humans along with Tepeu. Kukulkan was worshipped by many Mayans across history, especially in the Itza state, northern Yucatán Peninsula, where he was worshipped, and his cult made for the state religion. His worship aside, many folk tales about Kukulkan were passed along from one generation of Mayans to the other.

In one version of Kukulkan's origin, he was a young boy who turned into a serpent. Sometimes known as the plumed serpent, Kukulkan's sister looked after him, staying in a cave. As the years went by, he kept growing bigger and bigger until the cave could no longer hold him, and his sister couldn't feed him anymore. Kukulkan eventually burst out of the cave and flew into the sea, causing an earthquake in the process. The Mayans say that Kukulkan caused an earthquake in July of every year just to let his sister know that he is still alive and well.

Another folk tale claims that Kukulkan was a massive, winged serpent that flew directly into the sun, attempting to speak to it. The sun was too proud, though, and it wouldn't speak with the winged serpent, and it burned his tongue. This story bears some resemblance to the tragedy of Icarus in Greek mythology, who flew too close to the sun.

Kukulkan now travels before the rain god Chaac, his tail moving and sweeping the earth clean in anticipation of the rain. In a Lacandon Maya variation of that tale, Kukulkan is an evil serpent and a pet of the sun god.

His origins aside, the Mayans owe a great debt of gratitude to Kukulkan. He is said to have had some sort of power over knowledge and wisdom, and in some stories, he was the deity responsible for blessing humans with writing and laws. In some myth variations, Kukulkan took human form and was praised and revered as a fearless warrior. It is said that as a human, he later morphed into a serpent. Many of his Mayan worshippers believed that Kukulkan was responsible for their power, which is why you can find several statues and paintings of a feathered serpent, but instead of its head, there is a Mayan warrior's head. In other versions, the warrior comes out of the serpent's head, as a way to honor and show how Kukulkan gave the Mayans power.

In short, Kukulkan is thought to have been the creator of humans and the god responsible for their evolution as a species and for spreading knowledge and wisdom among mankind. You'll often find his name associated with art, medicine, architecture, and all other endeavors that make a civilization, and the Mayans loved and worshipped him for it.

Ah-Mun

We've talked earlier about the significance of maize in Mayan culture, the material from which the gods shaped mankind. In the pantheon of Mayan gods, Ah-Mun is the personification of maize and is sometimes referred to as the maize god. In some depictions, a cob of corn grows from Ah-Mun's head. He was also the god of agriculture and fertility, a youthful god responsible for providing the Maya with food and crops.

Ah-Mun is sometimes depicted in glorious combat with the death god Ah Puch himself, but that was mostly in the pre-Columbian era. Speaking of different periods of Mayan civilization, maize was often depicted as a woman during later Mayan oral narratives, not much unlike wheat in Greek mythology. But before the Spanish conquest, maize was depicted as a god, Ah-Mun. We will talk later about the importance of a maize god, not just in mankind's creation myths but also in cosmological creation myths. Ah-Mun was also worshipped as a god of protection, and many Mayans prayed to him, asking for protection from the evils of the world.

Huracan

Huracan's role in Mayan mythology is complicated and bears different interpretations, starting from the creation of humans. He was a god of storms and chaos, the deity responsible for natural catastrophes. Huracan could summon natural elements like wind, earth, and fire, using them to cause storms, rain, and other disasters. Huracan dwelled in the vast sky, and he played a major role in the creation of humans. Many Mayans believe that he sent the great flood that destroyed one of the failed attempts at making humans. He was there from the start, involved in the different phases of creation. After the flood, it was Huracan who beckoned the earth to rise out of the sea. He invoked the mountains and lands to rise until they were visible again from the surface of the planet.

In Mayan culture, Huracan was often shown to be a one-legged god—in some versions, that leg turned into a serpent. In the Popol Vuh, it is said that Huracan was the one that roamed the earth in search of new materials to make new humans. He found corn and turned it into a dough, out of which the four first men were created, and gives the names Jaguar Quitze, Dark Jaguar, Not Right Now, and Jaguar Night. It is also believed that it was Huracan that limited the human's super abilities and took their ability to see across oceans and even fly.

Despite his massive role in the creation of mankind, Huracan's role in later Mayan civilization was somewhat diminished. He was worshipped only as a god of storm and wind, with not many followers. Some scholars believe that the word 'hurricane' is derived from Huracan's name, a word we still use today that means a massive storm. Still, Huracan was feared and respected due to his powerful abilities and ability to control nature's elements. Moreover, he is also said to have been able to speak to inanimate objects—he commanded pans, mortars, and stones the ability to speak and commanded them to destroy the manikins that were created by the gods in a failed attempt to make humans.

Huracan's role in early Mayan civilization is thought to have been bigger since the early Mayans settled in areas where storms were fierce before the establishment of major cities and structures. It makes sense, then, that he was held in high regard at that time because he had the power to protect the people from terrible storms and fierce winds. As time went by, the Mayans built massive cities with sturdy buildings that rendered them safe from storms and winds, which is why Huracan's role diminished in Mayan culture, and some Mayans began viewing him as a lesser god.

Ah-Puch

Like all major civilizations across human history, the Mayans feared and revered death, and they had a deity for it. That deity was the god of death, Ah-Puch, one of the most powerful deities in the whole Mayan pantheon. Ah-Puch, however, wasn't just the god of death, darkness, and disaster. He was also the god of regeneration, beginnings, and in some versions, childbirth. The K'iche' people believed that Ah-Puch was the ruler of Metnal, the underworld in the Mayan culture. The Yucatec Maya, on the other hand, believed that he was only one of the rulers or lords of Xibalba, which is another word for Metnal, rather than the supreme ruler.

Ah-Puch's portrayal was often rather grim as his stature would impose. He was usually shown as a skeletal figure with bulging ribs and a death's head skull—sometimes, the head was an owl's head due to Ah-Puch's association with owls. On other occasions, he was shown as a bloated figure in a late stage of decomposition. He was also often depicted wearing bells, much like his Aztec counterpart Mictlantecuhtli. There are quite a few similarities between Aztec and Mayan cultures due to their proximity and the fact that the peoples of those regions shared many similarities and historical traditions. For example, the Mayans and Aztecs associated death with dogs and owls, which is why Ah-Puch was often depicted with one or the other.

One of Ah-Puch's names was Cizin, which was often shown as a dancing skeleton with a cigarette. Cizin wore a terrifying collar of human eyes around his neck, each dangling from the nerve cords in a gruesome display of death. They called him the 'stinking one' since he had a foul smell, as death should and the fact that his name meant flatulence or stench. There are many similarities between Ah-Puch or Cizin and the devil in Christianity. Both trapped the evil souls and sinners in the underworld where they were tormented and suffered for eternity as punishment for their crimes.

Ah-Puch was associated with a lot of carnage and destruction as the god of death. He was shown plucking the trees from the roots planted by another Mayan god, Chap, the rain god. He is also depicted in Mayan culture with the god of war killing humans or sacrificing them. It isn't surprising that Ah-Puch is associated with the god of war since he ruled Metnal, the lowest level in the Mayan underworld. He was also associated with the gods of disease and sacrifice. Ah-Puch was an antithesis of fertility in some Mayan folk tales and is shown as scheming and conspiring against the gods of fertility.

Like most people, the Mayans feared death, which is why Ah-Puch was held in high regard and feared. Some scholars even claim that the Mayans had a bigger fear of death than other Mesoamerican cultures. This can be felt in their depiction of Ah-Puch, who is said to hunt the injured and the sick, stalking their houses to steal their souls. This depiction as a hunting figure, ruthless and conniving, shows how the Mayans dreaded Ah-Puch rather than revered him. The Mayan rituals of mourning the dead often entailed loud wails and extreme mourning rituals that were believed to drive and scare Ah-Puch away and stop him from taking any more loved ones into his underworld domain. The explanation for this is Ah-Puch thinks you're tormented by one of his lesser demons if you howl or scream, so he lets you go.

Chaac

The god of rain, Chaac, was worshipped by many in the Yucatan region and was very popular among the regional Mayans. He is said to be the brother of the sun god Kinich Ahau, and the two brothers were supposedly tortured by their adoptive parents, who were unkind. However, Chaac and his brother eventually managed to trick and defeat them. Unfortunately, Chaac betrayed his brother not long after that and had an affair with his wife. For this, he suffered a great punishment, and the rain that falls from the sky is said to be Chaac's tears for his crime.

In other variations of the myth, Chaac is shown with a lightning ax that he used to strike the sky, cracking the clouds open to making the rainfall. Chaac is also often shown with fangs and reptilian scales, but that wasn't the only way he was depicted. Like many Mayan gods with more than one form, Chaac had four, one for each cardinal direction. Every one of the directions of the world corresponded to a side of Chaac's personality and color. Chaak Xib Chaac was the Red Chaac of the East, Sak Xib Chaac was the White Chaac of the North, Ex Xib Chaac was the Black Chaac of the West, and the last is Kan Xib Chaac, the Yellow Chaac of the South. Together, they were called the Chaacs, and they were worshipped as gods by the Mayans. Each of those four Chaacs is said to have a different role in a fire ritual that was held to bring rain. One of them takes the first, the second starts it, the third gives it shape, and the fourth put it out. With the fire lit, the ritual entailed throwing hearts of animals into the fire as a sacrifice while four Chaac priests would pour water into the flames from jugs. The Mayans performed this ritual twice a year during the wet and dry seasons.

Chaac played a huge role in the Mayans' lives because of his control over the rain, which was integral to the people's survival. Without rain, they wouldn't be able to grow their crops, and they would starve. With Chaac's blessing, rain would fall from the sky and help them grow their crops. This is also why Chaac is associated with maize, which, as mentioned several times, was a very important part of the Mayan diet. Chaac didn't live in the sky despite his association with rain, unlike other rain gods in different civilizations. He instead dwelled in the earth in places where water flows in caves and cenotes. Some ancient paintings show him with a wide mouth to symbolize a cave opening. He was also often shown with a curling nose.

Ceremonies and rituals were made to honor Chaac and ask for his blessing more than many other Mayan gods because of how much the people needed him. Sometimes, it went as far as sacrificing young boys and girls to appease the rain god, but that often happened during desperate times when the people have suffered a drought for a long time. There are other documented rituals where people were tossed into the sacred cenote of Chichén Itzá along with precious stones of jade and gold, all to appease Chaac and ask for his help. Archaeologists found proof of other ceremonies that didn't involve human sacrifice. Either way, the number of rituals and ceremonies dedicated to Chaac gives us an idea of how important he was to the Mayan people and his role in their lives.

Bacabs

The Mayans called the four gods of winds and directions Bacabs, the deities holding the four corners of the world. They were also the gods of the interior of the earth and its water deposits. The Bacabs were supposedly four brothers (Cantzicnal, Saccimi, Hosanek, and Hobnil) placed on earth at the time of creation at the four points of the world, carrying the sky so it wouldn't fall on the earth. They managed to escape with the great flood. For the Yucatec Maya, the Bacabs were also known as Muluc, Kan, Ix, and Cauac. The first two were responsible for positive energy in the world, while the latter two generated negative energy. The gods used this contrast between positive and negative energies to create humans and the world itself. In Yucatan and older depictions, the Bacabs were shown as old men lifting the 'sky-dragon.' Their portrayal often showed some animal features and attributes like a turtle, snail, conch, bee, or spider web.

As mentioned in the Chilam Balam, the Bacabs played an important role after the nine gods of the night captured the thirteen gods of the day with the help of Ah Muzen Cab. According to the Mayan text of Chilam Balam, "then the sky would fall, it would fall down, it would fall down upon the earth, when the four gods, the four Bacabs, were set up, who brought about the destruction of the world." They undid what happened and shaped the world how they pleased. In some versions of Mayan mythology, the Bacabs (sometimes referred to as a single or unitary concept) were the sons of the creator god Itzamna and the goddess Ixchebelyax.

Over the years and different Mayan generations, the Bacabs were honored through a series of rituals and ceremonies. Each of the four was given a corner of the earth and was designated a year bearer day (basically a new year day). Cantzicnal was in the north, bearing the color white, and associated with the year Muluc. Hobnil was east, red, and given the year, Kan. Hosanek was south, yellow, and Cauac. Saccimi was west, black, and Ix. You'll notice that these are the names given to them by the Yucatan Maya, which might have had an origin during a past time of the Mayan calendar.

The Bacabs were also associated with rain and farming, and they were closely connected to the four Chaacs, the rain god. They were associated with the wind deities Pauahtuns as well. Due to their role as New Year harbingers, the Bacabs played a significant role in ceremonies, particularly divination ceremonies, and were often invoked with matters of the weather, crops, and bees. They were also invoked in curing rituals.

Hun Hunahpu

Hun Hunahpu is another central figure in Mayan mythology. He is the father of the Hero Twins Xbalanque and Hunahpu (or Head-Apu). The story of the Hero Twins is one of the most popular in Mayan mythology, and it tells of two brothers who accomplished great things, including avenging their father, who was beheaded in the underworld by some of its lords. The twins were born to the virgin goddess Xquic, which happened when the severed head of Hun Hunahpu spit into her hands in the underworld from a calabash tree.

While his story sometimes varies in Mayan mythology, Hun Hunahpu is believed to have been a god of maize. Some sources back that theory, such as a pottery depiction of a cacao tree on the tonsured maize god. As a maize god, he was shown as handsome and young with a headdress of corn, his hair the silk of the corn itself. Hun Hunahpu's decapitation is believed to happen with the start of harvest, and he is reborn at the beginning of the new growing season. This meant that Hun Hunahpu was associated with maize for the ancient Mayans and rebirth and regeneration.

The Popol Vuh tells us that Hun Hunahpu was beheaded because the lords of the underworld saw him playing a ballgame with his brother, and they were annoyed and angered, so they summoned the two to Xibalba. The Mayans had a popular ballgame where two teams competed in shooting a solid rubber ball through a stone ring. Despite its popularity, it is believed that only a select few gods and men could play this game. Hun Hunahpu and his brother were met in the underworld with a series of traps and tricks designed to hurt them. And so, the lords of the underworld sacrificed the brothers and beheaded Hun Hunahpu when they failed the tests, hanging his head on a tree (cacao). It is said that Hun Hunahpu's twin sons were more skilled as ballplayers, and they went on to avenge their father's death. They were summoned to Xibalba just like their father and faced the same traps, but the twins were smart, and they ended up tricking the lords of the underworld, killing them, and reviving their father and uncle in the process.

Buluc-Chabtan

One of the most feared in the Mayan god pantheon, Buluc-Chabtan was the god of war, violence, death, and destruction—not to be confused with other deities of death as Buluc-Chabtan was the god of sudden death due to violence rather than natural death. He was the deity people prayed to before embarking on a battle or going to war, and they invoked his name when they wanted to avoid sudden death and stay safe. It was always a good idea to pray to and honor Buluc-Chabtan just to avoid incurring his wrath. Unfortunately, this also meant that many human sacrifices were offered to him. Human sacrifices were often given to the gods because the Mayans saw blood as nourishment for the gods, so nothing pleased the deities more than a human sacrifice. It's worth noting that virgin sacrifices were not welcomed, contrary to what is shown in movies. Prisoners of war were a much more convincing offering, and the Mayans more often used them to appease gods like Buluc-Chabtan. While beheading the human sacrifice was common in the early Mayan periods, heart removal was the more common practice later on.

Buluc-Chabtan is depicted in a gruesome light more often than not. He is sometimes shown to be eaten by maggots like in the Dresden Codices, one of the few remaining Mayan books. In terrifying imagery, Buluc-Chabtan is shown burning people alive on a spit that he used to stab them first or setting entire houses on fire and killing people. Buluc-Chabtan was associated with mayhem and carnage wherever he went, which is why he is often depicted with Ah Puch, the god of death.

The problem with Buluc-Chabtan is that not many stories survived about him except in some archaeological sites and a few surviving writings. However, it is believed that Buluc-Chabtan was one of the more evil gods that people avoided and feared rather than worshiped and revered. He was a god of human sacrifices to whom many were given in the hopes that he would keep his distance and spare the lives of his subjects.

Camazotz

Speaking of evil, unkind gods, Camazotz was the bat god of the underworld, which alone should give you an idea about his role in the Mayan culture. His name translates to 'death bat,' and he was considered a god of death, sacrifice, and the night itself. In Xibalba, he fed on blood and was the one who beheaded Hunahpu. Later on, he is defeated by the twin heroes when Hunahpu is revived, and they cast him out of creation.

Despite this, Camazotz is still mentioned in the Mayan religion today, and featured in the Popol Vuh. He is said to have a leaf-like nose, an anthropomorphized bat whose name evoked fear of darkness and the unknown. He is sometimes depicted with a sacrificial knife in one hand and a human head in the other. Camazotz tricked one of the brothers (Hunahpu) and ripped his head off when they faced the final test, giving it to the lords of the underworld to use as a ball for their amusement.

Camaxtli

Like many of the ancient peoples of Mesoamerica and the ancient world, the Mayans believed in fate and cared a great deal for it. Camaxtli is the god they worshipped as a deity for fate, and he was also a god of hunting, fire, and in some retellings, war. Camaxtli was also one of the creator gods, credited with creating life on earth and shaping the world as we know it today. Some versions of Mayan Mythology also credit him with bringing fire to the earth, similar to Prometheus in Greek Mythology.

Chen

Also known as Chin, she was the goddess of magic, maize, and the moon in some versions. Chen was also a patron of homosexuality and is often associated with homoeroticism in Mayan culture. Some tales claim that Chen introduced homosexuality to the Mayan nobles, who then went on to preach it to their children and encouraged them to be a part of homosexual marriages. Often depicted as a counselor of kings, Chen was sometimes shown with male genitals, especially if surrounded by demonic figures.

Ekchuah

As Mayan civilization evolved, trade became an important part of the culture, and there were trade routes that merchants had to cross to deliver products and goods. Those routes were often filled with dangers, whether human or natural. For that reason, the Mayans needed a god to protect travelers and merchants. Also known as God M, Ekchuah looked after not just travelers and merchants but also warriors. Ekchuah was also a patron of cacao and products derived from it. In Mayan interpretation, he was shown as a dark-skinned warrior with a bag over his shoulder and a spear. In other variations, he is black-and-white striped. His mouth is enclosed in red-brown skin, and he has two curved lines right of his eyes.

When travelers had a journey to cover, they would put three stones over each other and light incense to honor Ekchuah and pray that he protects them on their perilous journey. Ekchuah was also sometimes depicted in combat and battle along with gods of war, sacrifice, and death, which is believed to indicate the skills requirements for a merchant. They often had to know how to fight to protect themselves on the road against all dangers.

Chapter Three:

Heroes, Folk Tales, and Mayan Myths

In the Mayan pantheon, gods and goddesses weren't the only beings worthy of mention even centuries after those stories were told. Other mythical creatures played a significant role in Mayan folklore and heroes whose stories were worthy of song and praise across Mayan history. This chapter will look into those heroes and creatures and how they played into Mayan mythology. We will also explore some Mayan myths that helped shape the beliefs of the Mayans over several generations.

The Hero Twins

We briefly mentioned the Hero Twins earlier, and it's bound to be the first story about Mayan heroes you'll find in most sources. The story of the Mayan Hero Twins is a central part of the K'iche' people's history, and it is featured extensively in the

Popol Vuh. They were called Hunahpu and Xbalan-que, but those two weren't the first Hero Twins in Mayan mythology. As we mentioned earlier, their father was Hun Hunahpu (also known as 1 Hunter), whose brother was Vuqub Hunahpu (7 Hunter). The Mayan calendar was cyclical and entailed the world being destroyed by a cosmic event before regenerating again, so each period had its different heroes. Hun Hunahpu and his brother Vuqub Hunahpu lived during the second world of Mayan history.

It is said that Hun Hunahpu and his brother Vuqub Hunahpu were very skilled in the Mayan ballgame, but they were very noisy and loud when they played, which angered the lords of the underworld Xibalba. The brothers were invited to Xibalba by Lords One Death and Seven Death for a match. The brothers didn't suspect treachery, and so they went, but in Xibalba, a series of tests and tricks awaited them, designed to end their lives and put them to suffer. They first had to cross rivers of blood and spikes, and they did. Then they were asked to go through several other tests, and they failed some, like when the gods of the underworld asked the brothers to greet them by name, but the brothers faced wooden statues, and they didn't recognize the gods, which was a great transgression.

On the eve of the football game, the brothers were given torches and cigars and ordered to keep both lit throughout the night without consuming them, which the brothers naturally failed. The punishment for that failure was death. Hun Hunahpu and Vuqub Hunahpu were killed, and the former's head was cut off and put in the fork of a tree. They only buried his body with his brother. The lords of the underworld, though, didn't plan what happened next. The daughter of one of the lords of Xibalba named Xquic approached the calabash tree and saw Hun Hunahpu's head. The two talked, and Hun Hunahpu eventually spat into her hand, impregnating her.

Xquic fled from Xibalba and sought out Hun Hunahpu and Vuqub Hunahpu's mother, who reluctantly took her on and became her ward—though it is said that the mother set up several trials to have Xquic prove her identity. Nine months later, two more twins were born: Hunahpu and Xbalanque. It is believed that the twins' grandmother was not kind to them, and neither were their older half-brothers who disliked the newcomers. Their elder half-brothers were artisans and intellectuals who feared that the twin might steal their thunder and take some of their attention. At some point, the grandmother demanded Hunahpu and Xbalanque be removed the house because they cried a lot. The legend goes that the elder half-brothers took Hunahpu and Xbalanque to a hill where they planned on killing them, but they didn't succeed.

Hunahpu and Xbalanque grew up without much hatred for their spiteful family, and they were forced to work even as young boys, hunting birds to feed the family while their elder brothers played around. When it was time to eat, Hunahpu and Xbalanque ate last despite being the hunters. Despite their cruel upbringing, the brothers knew that their time would come, and they displayed immense wit from a young age. This was shown in the Popol Vuh when Hunahpu and Xbalanque returned one day from the hunt without any birds. This was met with hostility from the elder brothers. The young twins said they did indeed shoot the birds, but they fell into a tree and got caught in its branches, so they could not get them. The elder half-brothers begrudgingly went with the twins to the tree and started climbing up to retrieve the birds. They couldn't, though. The tree kept growing taller, and the older brothers were trapped.

Some believe this is a sign that the twin brothers had supernatural powers, which wouldn't be unreasonable since a god and goddess birthed them. It can also be that the gods blessed and helped Hunahpu and Xbalanque. To further humiliate his elder half-brothers, Hunahpu told them to take their loincloths off and use them to try and descend from the trees by tying them to their waists. The rope quickly turned into a tail, and the brothers were all turned into monkeys. The grandmother wanted them to return after Hunahpu and Xbalanque that they were not hurt. When they finally did, the grandmother laughed at their new form, and the monkeys/men ran away.

The gods noticed the twin brothers, and they were known to be special. This was shown when Huracan himself approached them with a problem. Seven Macaw (also known as Vucub Caquix) was a vain and arrogant god that the other deities disliked.

He claimed to be either the sun or the moon, strutting around with ornaments and false teeth made of gemstones. Huracan approached Hunahpu and Xbalanque to get their help defeating Seven Macaw. The brothers accepted Huracan's offer.

They first tried to kill Seven Macaw when he was having a meal on a tree, and they shot the vain god in the jaw with a blowgun. Seven Macaw fell off the tree, but he survived, suffering minor injuries. It is said then that Seven Macaw ripped off Hunahpu's arm as he was trying to escape. The twin brothers didn't despair, though, and they proved their wit once again. With the help of two gods in disguise, they approached Macaw again. The gods pretended to be Hunahpu's parents and approached Macaw, asking him to return the stolen arm. The disguised gods claimed they were poor and their grand-children's only family, trying to provide for them by working as doctors and dentists. This struck a nerve with Macaw, and he asked that they fix his teeth damaged by the blowgun shot. The Popol Vuh also mentions that he needed his eyes cured, but it's not specified what was wrong with them.

The grandparents/gods in disguise then removed his jeweled teeth and put white corn instead, and they also took out the ornaments surrounding his eyes. This stripped Macaw of his greatness, and he fell from grace. He supposedly died of shame not long after. He had two songs, though, and they were just as arrogant and vain as their father. They were called Zipacna and Cabrakan. The two told lies and claimed they were the creator and could destroy the earth if they were so pleased. The twins used another trick to vanquish Zipacna, the eldest of the two, burying him under a mountain. Cabrakan was a more challenging foe, and Huracan was forced to implore the twins' help again.

Cabrakan was arrogant and vain, and he claimed he could destroy mountains at will. The twins decided to use that against him. They told him of a mountain they had encountered in their travels that kept growing without limitation. Cabrakan was naturally intrigued and told them to lead him to the mountain. The brothers agreed and accompanied the god, but they were planning for his demise along the journey. As shown by their childhood, the twins were excellent hunters when they hunted birds to feed their family. Along the journey to the mountain that didn't exist, they shot birds down and roasted them whenever they stopped. Cabrakan became hungry, and his appetite grew upon seeing the brothers' roasted meals. He asked them for some, and they gave him a bird they had cooked with gypsum and plaster, which can poison a god. Cabrakan ate, and his body grew weak. Seizing the opportunity, the twin brothers tied him up, and Cabrakan's story ended with him being tossed into a hole in the earth where he remains buried.

Hunahpu and Xbalanque also liked to play ball like their father and uncle. They played in the same courtyard and their noise disturbed the lords of Xibalba, who were just as annoyed as they were with the previous twins. They sent word to Hunahpu and Xbalanque to come to the underworld and play a ballgame in the lords' own court. Despite their grandmother's attempt to sway them and hide the message, the boy got it and decided to travel to Xibalba to play ball with the lords of the underworld. Their grandmother feared they would suffer the same fate as their father and uncle, but the boys traveled still.

Much the same as their father and uncle, the twins faced a series of tests and tricks in their journey to the underworld. These were set to embarrass and shame them but Hunahpu and Xbalanque were smart, and they would not fall prey to any of those traps. One of the first and biggest transgressions their father and uncle had done was not recognizing the gods and mistaking the wooden manikins for the lords of the underworld. To work around that, Hunahpu and Xbalanque sent a mosquito before their arrival to help them figure out which gods were real and which were wooden. By the time they arrived at Xibalba, it was much easier to recognize who the real gods were.

Another trap the lords of the underworld had prepared was setting up a bench for visitors that was actually a heated stone used for cooking. Hunahpu and Xbalanque were wise to the trap, and they declined the gods' invitation to sit on the visitors' bench. The gods grew frustrated with the brothers' ability to see through the traps, and they ordered them to leave for the Dark House, where the first of the deadly tests awaited. The twins survived the tests that had got their father and uncle.

They managed to last the night without consuming the torch or the cigarette. They tricked the lords of Xibalba by using a macaw's tail and disguising it as a torch. They put fireflies at the ends of their cigars to make it look like the cigars were kept alight all night long. The gods' frustration only grew, and they decided to skip the remaining tests and invited the twins directly to play the ballgame they had supposedly come for.

The lords of Xibalba used a ball with blades in it, designed to kill the twins, who were on to the gods' trickery.In some interpretations, the ball was made of a skull and covered in crushed bones, which would've been just as deadly. Hunahpu stopped the ball with a racquet, revealing to all the trickery of the gods. The brothers were disgruntled and showed their dismay by threatening to leave the game since they only came to be killed as it seemed. The gods accepted a compromise and allowed the game to be played with the twins' own rubber ball. The twins played a long and intense game against the Lords of Xibalba.

The twins let the gods win on purpose as a part of their plan to defeat the gods in their own game.

Since they lost the game, Hunahpu and Xbalanque were sent to a place called the Razor House (the second of the deadly tests after the Dark House), which was filled with lethal knives that had a will of their own and moved freely inside the place. The twins talked with the knives and convinced them to stop moving. This ruined the test for the gods, and it didn't stop there. As a reward for their victory, the gods demanded an impossible gift: petals from the guarded gardens of Xibalba. The brothers, however-er, were prepared, and they sent leaf-cutting ants to the garden that easily slipped past the guards and stole the petals.

In a rematch of the ballgame, the brothers let themselves lose again to the lords of Xibalba. As punishment, they were sent to the following test, the Cold House. They defeated this test and kept on losing one ballgame after the other so they could be put through the other tests like Fire House and Jaguar House, which they defeated with their wit and steadiness. With each test they passed, the gods of Xibalba grew more furious. They sent the brothers eventually to the Bat House. This was when Hunahpu made the mistake of peeking to see if the dead bats were still around and if daylight had come. This was when Camazotz beheaded him. Extremely pleased with Hunahpu's defeat and beheading, the gods used his head as a ball for a while, but Xbalanque still survived. With the help of some beasts, he made a replacement head for his brother until the two managed to replace the gods' new ball with a gourd. They then retrieved Hunahpu's head and put it back, striking another shameful defeat to the gods of the underworld.

This was one defeat too many for the gods, whose patience had reached its end. They ordered a great oven to be built, and they summoned the twins again so they could trick them into entering the oven where they would finally meet their end. Hunahpu and Xbalanque realized that this final trick was meant to end their lives, but they stepped into the oven and let the gods burn and kill them, turning their bodies into ashes. Overjoyed after finally vanquishing the stubborn twins, the gods of Xibalba threw the twins' ashes into a river. It turned out, though, that this was a part of the twins' plans all along.

In the river, Hunahpu and Xbalanque's bodies regenerated. First, they returned as catfish, and then, later on, they were fully restored as young boys once again. As young boys, the lords of Xibalba couldn't recognize the twins, and they were allowed to dwell in the underworld. Revived, the twins had the power of the gods then. They could set fire to people or homes and then bring them back from ashes. They could kill or sacrifice one another and then return from the dead. Words of their miracles spread across Xibalba, and the lords of the underworld invited the twins to their court to entertain them and perform miracles or dance for them.

Hunahpu and Xbalanque gracefully accepted the offer and performed their tricks and miracles for the gods for free. The gods still couldn't recognize the young boys who claimed to be orphans. The twins began performing their usual tricks. They killed beasts and brought them back to life, burned the lords' houses, and restored them from ashes. For a finale to their performance, Xbalanque killed Hunahpu, cutting him into pieces. He then restored Hunahpu from the dead. The lords of the underground were so impressed that the most powerful of them, One Death and Seven Death, demanded that this trick be performed upon them. The Hero Twins gladly accepted and killed the highest lords of Xibalba, but they never restored them from the dead.

This was when Hunahpu and Xbalanque declared their identity to the remaining lords, shocking them. They told the gods of Xibalba not just that they were the two youths they had killed and tossed into a river not too long ago, but that they were also the sons of Hun Hunahpu whom the gods had betrayed and tricked many years earlier. The gods were stunned and admitted their crimes, pleading for mercy. The brothers Hunahpu and Xbalanque had won. As punishment for the treacherous lords of the underworld, Xibalba was no longer a realm to be revered and worshipped. It was no longer the great underworld, and the Mayan people living on earth would no longer offer sacrifices and offerings to the lords of the underworld. Xibalba was vanquished, soon to be forgotten.

Relieved to have finally avenged their father and uncle, the twins retrieved their father's remains and left Xibalba to return to earth. Their journey didn't end on earth, though. They climbed further up to the sky where they resided there as the lords of the sky, one of them becoming the sun and the other the moon. The story of the Hero Twins was one of the most popular in Mayan history, and it is one whose effect spans other Mesoamerican cultures.

Mythical Creatures and Places

Like most ancient cultures, several mythical creatures and folk tales surrounded the Mayan civilization. Some of them are shared with other Mesoamerican cultures, and others are unique.

Sisemite: In Mayan folklore, Sisemite was a large and scary creature like bigfoot in urban folktales. It dwelled in the wilderness and is described as powerful and tall, a shaggy beast that often takes a humanoid form. The Sisemite is said to sometimes steal women or children, keeping them prisoners in his cave. If he captures a man, he feasts on its flesh and blood, crushing the bones in his teeth. The creature doesn't speak in Mayan myths, communicating only in howls or screams.

Alux: The Alux are magical people for the Yucatan Maya, thought to be small in stature and are thought to have been invisible, though they were said to manifest to talk with or scare humans or to congregate. They are tricksters that are often associated with caves, forests, and fields. The Alux are generally considered benevolent, but their wrath can be terrible, which is why they were treated with reverence in Mayan culture.

Wayobs (Ways): The plural of Way, the Wayobs are protective spirits who have powerful energies that can help people navigate the energy of a certain day and of life itself. It is said that the Wayobs or Ways manifest as animals to guide people (or harm them), which is why they were often considered totems or totemic guides. Some Mayans believed that a person had a Way that they could connect with through dreams in the 'dreaming place,' where the Way can direct you and guide you in life.

Witzob: This is what Olympus was to the Greek gods. Witzob is the holy mountain of the gods where they dwelled, but it was not considered an inanimate rock but rather a living being with powerful spiritual energy. The Mayans, in general, cared a great deal about mountains as they were considered symbols of great power and spiritual growth due to their imposing heights.

World Tree (Ceiba): The world tree wasn't just mentioned in Norse Mythology. The Mayans had Ceiba, the tree of life whose roots stretch into the underworld, its body grows in the middle world, which is earth, and its branches blossom in paradise.

The Universe for the Mayans

The universe was multilayered for the Mayans, consisting of layers that spanned the underworld, middle world, and paradise. The heaven or paradise consisted of 13 layers above the earth, supported by the Bacabs at the four corners, while the earth rested on the back of a turtle floating in the ocean. There were 9 layers of Xibalba beneath the earth, the underworld where the evil was sent as punishment. The world tree (Ceiba) linked those layers together, and the spirits—and even gods—traveled along this tree to move between heaven, hell, and earth. A bird god named Itzam-Ye dwells in the axis of Ceiba, and he is the deity that knows the secrets of all planes of existence. The thirteen layers of heaven were ruled by thirteen gods known as the Oxlahuntiku, while the lords of death or gods the underworld Xibalba were 9 and called Bolontiku.

As mentioned earlier, the Mayan priests viewed time as never-ending, consisting of major successions of cycles with no defined beginning or end. Time itself was considered holy and divine by the Mayans, and all-time cycles were believed to be gods. Despite these notions, the Mayans believed the world in its current form is doomed to end in a cataclysm, as former worlds have done before it, so that a new cycle could begin. This ensures the eternal succession of cycles so that time can repeat itself. Based on this notion, Mayan priests made predictions of the future by examining the past and trying to think of how the next cycle will end. In 2012, there was a widespread belief that the world would end according to the Mayan calendar since 2012 marked the end of the 5,126-year cycle. And this event was celebrated in several countries where Mayan culture still lingers.

Conclusion

The Mayan culture is one of the most interesting and fascinating to behold, with countless exciting stories and a rich history that spanned a massive region for centuries. The Mayan pantheon of gods includes hundreds of gods and goddesses revered and worshipped for a long time—some still are. Examining the Mayan mythology and folklore from different angles will show us the similarities between Mayan civilization and other Mesoamerican cultures. Yet, the Mayans were distinct in their view of the world and how they viewed divine figures.

The Mayan culture's incredible feats span everything from the arts to the sciences. This was a civilization that cared greatly for knowledge. Each province in a Mayan State had a high priest that taught in schools and helped younger generations gain the necessary knowledge and wisdom to grow to be leaders and thinkers. It is said that priesthood was hereditary for the Mayans, which shows the weight of such a massive responsibility to be not just a priest for a god but a teacher of generations and a spreader of knowledge.

The Mayans were dedicated in their rituals to honor the gods, going extreme lengths at times. Sacrifices aside, rituals and rites often included fasting and sexual abstinence, which are rituals practiced by other religions to day. If you look, you can find similarities between Mayan culture and religious practices in other religions, proof that the Mayans influenced countless peoples and civilizations even after the fall of the Mayan civilization. However, Mayan religion distinguished itself even from other Mesoamerican civilizations by the emphasis and refinement of mathematics and astronomical knowledge. The Mayans used this knowledge to honor the gods and create special temples to honor them as the Temple of Kukulcán.

Scholars believe that even the wisest and smartest of Aztec priests could not rival a Mayan priest, and the Aztecs could never come up with a concept as intricate and fascinating as the eternity of time and the repetition of cycles. It wouldn't be an overstatement to say that Mayans worshipped time, perhaps because they understood its importance and its role in the evolution of civilizations.

The Mayan civilization eventually crumbled like most great ones do, partly because of western invasion. The Mayan culture itself began to atrophy and decay over the later generations, which also afflicts many great civilizations toward the end. Fortunately, some surviving accounts of the Mayan mythology and folklore give us the incredible tales of great heroes and cunning gods that helped shape the world as we know it today.

References

Acan. (n.d.). Retrieved from Fandom.com website: https://mythus.fandom.com/wiki/Acan

Acat. (n.d.). Retrieved from Mayansandtikal.com website: https://mayansandtikal.com/mayan-gods/acat/

AH CUXTAL - the Lacandon God of Childbirth (Maya mythology). (n.d.). Retrieved from Godchecker.com website: https://www.godchecker.com/maya-mythology/AH-CUXTAL/

Ah Mun | Mayan deity. (n.d.). In Encyclopedia Britannica.

Ah-Bolom-Tzacab - Ah Bolom Tzacab is the leaf-nosed god of agriculture, but he also goes by a plethora of other names Ah Bolon Dz'acab Bolon Dzacab Bolon. (n.d.). Retrieved from Coursehero.com website: https://www.coursehero.com/file/58502476/Ah-Bolom-Tzacab/

Appleton, M. (2015). Mayan civilization: A beginners guide. North Charleston, SC: Createspace Independent Publishing Platform.

aprilholloway. (2013, January 30). The Maya myth of creation. Retrieved from Ancient-origins. net website: https://www.ancient-origins.net/ human-origins-folklore/maya-myth-creation-0063

Aztec and Maya myths: Karl A. taube: Free download, borrow, and streaming: Internet archive. (n.d.). Retrieved from Archive.org website: https:// archive.org/details/aztecmayamyths00taub/page/ n81/mode/2up

Camaxtli. (n.d.). Retrieved from Academickids.com website: https://academickids.com/encyclopedia/ index.php/Camaxtli

Camazotz: The Mayan bat god. (n.d.). Retrieved from Historicalmx.org website: https://historicalmx.org/ items/show/90

Cline, A. (n.d.-a). Ah Mucen Cab in the Mayan Religion. Retrieved from Learnreligions. com website: https://www.learnreligions.com/ ah-mucen-cab-god-of-bees-and-honey-250379

Cline, A. (n.d.-b). Ah Puch - Mayan god of death. Retrieved from Learnreligions.com website: https://www.learnreligions.com/ah-puch-ah-puch-god-of-death-250381

Cline, A. (n.d.-c). Buluc Chabtan: Mayan god of war. Retrieved from Learnreligions. com website: https://www.learnreligions.com/buluc-chabtan-buluc-chabtan-god-of-war-250382

Creation story of the Maya. (n.d.). Retrieved from Nmai.si.edu website: https://maya.nmai.si.edu/the-maya/creation-story-maya

Currie, S. (Ed.). (2012). Mayan mythology: Mayan mythology. Retrieved from https://www.cs.mcgill.ca/~rwest/wikispeedia/wpcd/wp/m/Maya_mythology.htm

Dundes, A. (1992). The Flood Myth (A. Dundes, Ed.). Berkeley, CA: University of California Press.

Huracan. (n.d.). Retrieved from Mayansandtikal.com website: https://mayansandtikal.com/mayan-gods/huracan/

Ketch, K. (2019, March 4). Ah Puch, god of death, darkness, and disaster. Retrieved from Kelseyketch.

com website: https://kelseyketch.com/2019/03/04/ah-puch-god-of-death-darkness-and-disaster/

Kris Hirst, K. (n.d.). Maya goddess of the moon, fertility, and death, ix Chel. Retrieved from Thoughtco.com website: https://www.thoughtco.com/ix-chel-mayan-goddess-moon-fertility-death-171592

Kukulkan. (2020, January 29). Retrieved from Gods-and-goddesses.com website: https://www.gods-and-goddesses.com/mayan/kukulkan/

Maestri, N. (n.d.-a). The curly-nosed Mayan rain god chaac had ancient Mesoamerican roots. Retrieved from Thoughtco.com website: https://www.thoughtco.com/chaac-ancient-maya-god-of-rain-lightning-and-storms-171593

Maestri, N. (n.d.-b). The Mayan myth of the hero twins - stories from the Popol Vuh. Retrieved from Thoughtco.com website: https://www.thoughtco.com/hunahpu-xbalanque-maya-hero-twins-171590

Mark, J. J. (2012). The Mayan pantheon: The many gods of the Maya. World History Encyclopedia.

Retrieved from https://www.worldhistory.org/ article/415/the-mayan-pantheon-the-many-gods-of-the-maya/

Maya legends (folklore, myths, and traditional Mayan Indian stories). (n.d.). Retrieved from Native-languages.org website: http://www.native-languages.org/maya-legends.htm

Maya stories of creation. (2014, November 3). Retrieved from Samnoblemuseum.ou.edu website: https://samnoblemuseum.ou.edu/collections-and-research/ethnology/mayan-textiles/ mayan-textiles-background/mayan-history/ creation/

Mayan creation myth by Megan wren. (n.d.). Retrieved from Utexas.edu website: http://www. laits.utexas.edu/doherty/plan2/wren.html

Mayan Gods and their stories. (2021, May 25). Retrieved from Mayamaya.ch website: https://www.mayamaya.ch/blog/stories-9/post/ mayan-gods-and-their-stories-229

Micky Bumbar (Lords of the Drinks). (2017, October 6). Acan and balche; alcohol in the ancient Mayan civilization. Retrieved from Lordsofthedrinks.com website: https://lordsofthedrinks.com/2017/10/06/acan-and-balche-alcohol-in-the-ancient-mayan-civilization/

No title. (n.d.). Retrieved from Study.com website: https://study.com/academy/lesson/chaac-mayan-god-of-rain-lightning-mythology-facts.html

pre-Columbian civilizations - Cosmology. (n.d.). In Encyclopedia Britannica.

Teaching History with 100 Objects - The Maya maize god. (n.d.). Retrieved from Teachinghistory100.org website: http://www.teachinghistory100.org/objects/about_the_object/maize_god

The Editors of Encyclopedia Britannica. (2009). Bacab. In Encyclopedia Britannica.

The Editors of Encyclopedia Britannica. (2018). Itzamná. In Encyclopedia Britannica.

The Museum Journal. (n.d.). Retrieved from Penn. museum website: https://www.penn.museum/sites/journal/416/

(N.d.). Retrieved from Sch.uk website: https://www.our-lady.lincs.sch.uk/_documents/%5B504554%5Dt2-h-4252-maya-civilization-creation-story-comprehension-activity-sheets-_ver_2.pdf